Growth Mindset Journal

Tweens & Teens

Why a growth mindset?

Because life has its up and downs and it's how you rise up to the challenges that define who you are. Growing up as a teenager today can be tough.

The best lessons in life aren't always taught at school. We aren't always taught how to cope with the speed bumps and curve balls that come our way.

This book is designed to help you build a growth mindset that's ready to take on whatever comes your way.

It's inspired by Christine, my teen sister.

Growth vs fixed mindset

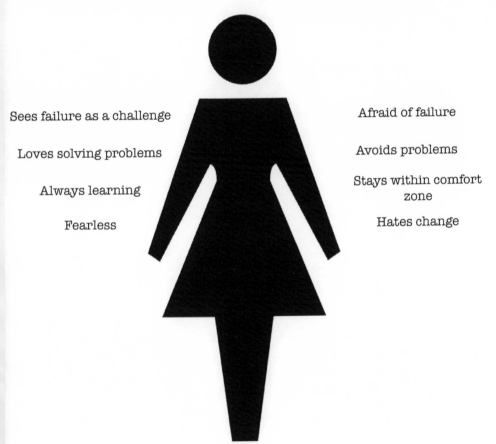

Sees failure as a challenge

Loves solving problems

Always learning

Fearless

Afraid of failure

Avoids problems

Stays within comfort zone

Hates change

Anyone who has never made a mistake has never tried anything new - Albert Einstein

Date: ___/___/_____

I believe I can train my brain to do
anything because...

_____

_____

_____

_____

_____

_____

_____

If I knew I wouldn't fail, I would...

_____

_____

_____

_____

_____

_____

Date: ___/___/_____

A list of things I'm great at...

_____

_____

_____

_____

_____

_____

A list of things I'd like to learn...

_____

_____

_____

_____

_____

_____

Date: ___/___/_____

To me failure means...

_____

_____

_____

_____

_____

_____

_____

I will not be afraid to fail because...

_____

_____

_____

_____

_____

_____

_____

If you want to find success,
double your rate of failure.
Unknown

Date: ___/___/_____

When I come across a challenge I...

_____

_____

_____

_____

_____

_____

Next time I come across a challenge, I will...

_____

_____

_____

_____

_____

_____

Date: ___/___/_____

What negative things do I say about myself?

_____

_____

_____

_____

_____

_____

_____

What can I say about myself instead?

_____

_____

_____

_____

_____

_____

_____

Date: ___/___/_____

When someone criticises me or gives me feedback I feel...

_____

_____

_____

_____

_____

_____

_____

What can I use criticism and feedback to improve instead?

_____

_____

_____

_____

_____

_____

Don't let other people's opinions control you. You are not a robot.
Uchenna Llo

Date: ___/___/_____

Think about a previous challenge you've
faced. How did you handle it?

_____

_____

_____

_____

_____

_____

_____

_____

_____

_____

_____

_____

_____

Date: ___/___/_____

What did you learn today outside of school?

_____

_____

_____

_____

_____

_____

_____

What would you like to get better at?

_____

_____

_____

_____

_____

_____

Date: ___/___/_____

What did you do today that made you think hard?

_____

_____

_____

_____

_____

_____

_____

_____

_____

_____

_____

_____

_____

_____

Dreams don't work
until you do
John C. Maxwell

What can I say to myself?

Instead of...	Try thinking...
I'm not good at this	What can I do to improve?
I failed	What have I learned from this?
This is hard work	
I don't have what it takes	
Other people do it so much better than me	
I've been told I shouldn't do this	
Maybe I should just give up	

Date: ___/___/_____

Think of a time when you were very
stressed. What caused it?

_____

_____

_____

_____

_____

_____

_____

How did you deal with the stress?

_____

_____

_____

_____

_____

_____

On handling stress

It's normal to feel stressed at various points in
our lives. Whether it's an important assignment
or changes in your home or school environment,
stress can come in many forms.

Whatever it is, know that you can use stress as
an opportunity to grow. People who've nailed the
art of managing stress are some of the most
resilient people I know.

Whenever you feel stressed, take deep breaths.

When you inhale, think of all the things troubling
you. Release your worries and fear as you
exhale.

Life is an experiment - Ralph Waldo Emerson

Draw this

You can be anyone and do anything if you put your mind to it. With this in mind, draw your dream life.

Every accomplishment
starts with the decision to
try.
Unknown

Date: ___/___/_____

Think of something you've always wanted to do. Now imagine doing it. If it didn't work out, what's the worse thing that could happen?

_____

_____

_____

_____

_____

_____

_____

_____

_____

_____

_____

_____

_____

Half empty or half full?

Imagine this circle as a glass of water.
Is it half empty or half full?
Discuss with a friend or family.

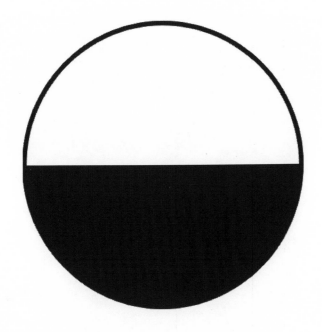

Date: ___/___/_____

Think of a time when things didn't go your way. How did you react?

_____

_____

_____

_____

_____

_____

_____

Knowing that it's ok to fail, how would you have reacted differently?

_____

_____

_____

_____

_____

Success is the ability to go
from one failure to another
with no loss of enthusiasm.
Winston Churchill

Date: ___/___/_____

Think of your favourite athlete or role model. Think about the challenges or failures they've had to overcome in life. List them here.

_____

_____

_____

_____

_____

_____

_____

_____

_____

_____

_____

_____

_____

Date: ___/___/_____

Where there is success, there is often failure. How do you think your favourite people in life have overcome them?

_____

_____

_____

_____

_____

_____

_____

_____

_____

_____

_____

_____

Date: ___/___/_____

Fill in the blank and then discuss.
Failure is....

_____

_____

_____

_____

_____

_____

_____

_____

_____

_____

_____

_____

_____

We must get our hearts broken sometimes. This is a good sign, having a broken heart. It means we have tried for something.
Elizabeth Gilbert

The bucket list

Write down a list of everything you want to learn/do.
Don't hold back!

The travel list

Write down a list of all the places you want to go.

People to meet

Write down a list of all the people you want to meet.

If you shoot for the stars and hit the moon, it's OK. But you've got to shoot for something. A lot of people don't even shoot.
Confucius

Your vision board

If you can dream it, you can make it your reality.

Put your goals into a vision board. Cut out pictures from old magazines or books that inspire you.

Date: ___/___/_____

Find someone you admire.
Have a discussion with them about the
challenges they've had to overcome.

_____

_____

_____

_____

_____

_____

_____

_____

_____

_____

_____

_____

_____

Date: ___/___/_____

Think of one thing you'd like to change in
the world. How can you help?

_____

_____

_____

_____

_____

_____

_____

_____

_____

_____

_____

_____

_____

_____

_____

You may have to fight a
battle more than once to
win it.
Margaret Thatcher

Positive affirmations

Sometimes we all need a little pick me up. When you're feeling a little down or challenged, affirmations remind us just how much we're capable of.

Write down a few affirmations you can refer to when when you're not feeling great.

i.e. I am capable of doing anything I want.

I will never fail.

Date: ___/___/_____

Think of a time when you solved a
problem you thought was impossible.
Write it down here.

_____

_____

_____

_____

_____

_____

_____

How did you overcome the problem?

_____

_____

_____

_____

_____

_____

Draw this

What do you think the world will be like 30 years from now? Draw it.

Most of the important things in the
world have been accomplished by
people who have kept on trying
when there seem no hope at all.
Dale Carnegie

Taking notice of all your wins

When we place too much focus on our challenges and failures, we lose sight of all our 'wins', all the little challenges we overcome. The following pages are to help document all your wins!

This could be acing a difficult test, making it through gym class or making friends at a new school.

Write it all down!

Date: ___/___/_____

A small challenge I came across...

_____

_____

_____

_____

_____

_____

_____

How I overcame it...

_____

_____

_____

_____

_____

_____

_____

Date: ___/___/_____

A big challenge I came across...

_____

_____

_____

_____

_____

_____

_____

How I overcame it...

_____

_____

_____

_____

_____

_____

_____

Date: ___/___/_____

An unexpected challenge I came across...

_____

_____

_____

_____

_____

_____

_____

_____

How I overcame it...

_____

_____

_____

_____

_____

_____

_____

Date: ___/___/_____

An exciting challenge I came across...

_____

_____

_____

_____

_____

_____

_____

How I overcame it...

_____

_____

_____

_____

_____

_____

Kicking goals

A goal without a plan is just a wish. Use the following goal planners to map out exactly how you'll achieve your goals.

Remember, no goal is ever too big.

PROGRESS

WEEK 1
What I did this week to work on my goal:

WEEK 2
What I did this week to work on my goal:

WEEK 3
What I did this week to work on my goal:

WEEK 4
What I did this week to work on my goal:

I REACHED MY GOAL, SO I GET

_____

REACH THE GOAL!

My goal

_____

PROGRESS

WEEK 1

What I did this week to work on my goal:

WEEK 2

What I did this week to work on my goal:

WEEK 3

What I did this week to work on my goal:

WEEK 4

What I did this week to work on my goal:

I REACHED MY GOAL, SO I GET

_____

REACH THE GOAL!

My goal

_____

PROGRESS

WEEK 1
What I did this week to work on my goal:

WEEK 2
What I did this week to work on my goal:

WEEK 3
What I did this week to work on my goal:

WEEK 4
What I did this week to work on my goal:

I REACHED MY GOAL, SO I GET _____

REACH THE GOAL!

GOAL GOAL GOAL GOAL GOAL GOAL

My goal _____

PROGRESS

WEEK 1

What I did this week to work on my goal:

WEEK 2

What I did this week to work on my goal:

WEEK 3

What I did this week to work on my goal:

WEEK 4

What I did this week to work on my goal:

I REACHED MY GOAL, SO I GET

_____

REACH THE GOAL!

My goal

_____

PROGRESS

WEEK 1

What I did this week to work on my goal:

WEEK 2

What I did this week to work on my goal:

WEEK 3

What I did this week to work on my goal:

WEEK 4

What I did this week to work on my goal:

I REACHED MY GOAL, SO I GET

_____

REACH THE GOAL!

My goal

_____

PROGRESS

WEEK 1
What I did this week to work on my goal:

WEEK 2
What I did this week to work on my goal:

WEEK 3
What I did this week to work on my goal:

WEEK 4
What I did this week to work on my goal:

I REACHED MY GOAL, SO I GET _____

REACH THE GOAL!

My goal _____

GOAL GOAL GOAL GOAL GOAL GOAL

PROGRESS

WEEK 1
What I did this week to work on my goal:

WEEK 2
What I did this week to work on my goal:

WEEK 3
What I did this week to work on my goal:

WEEK 4
What I did this week to work on my goal:

I REACHED MY GOAL, SO I GET _____

REACH THE GOAL!

My goal _____

PROGRESS

WEEK 1
What I did this week to work on my goal:

WEEK 2
What I did this week to work on my goal:

WEEK 3
What I did this week to work on my goal:

WEEK 4
What I did this week to work on my goal:

I REACHED MY GOAL, SO I GET

_____

REACH THE GOAL!

My goal

_____

PROGRESS

WEEK 1

What I did this week to work on my goal:

WEEK 2

What I did this week to work on my goal:

WEEK 3

What I did this week to work on my goal:

WEEK 4

What I did this week to work on my goal:

I REACHED MY GOAL, SO I GET _____

REACH THE GOAL!

My goal _____

PROGRESS

WEEK 1
What I did this week to work on my goal:

WEEK 2
What I did this week to work on my goal:

WEEK 3
What I did this week to work on my goal:

WEEK 4
What I did this week to work on my goal:

I REACHED MY GOAL, SO I GET

_____

REACH THE GOAL!

My goal

_____

PROGRESS

WEEK 1

What I did this week to work on my goal:

WEEK 2

What I did this week to work on my goal:

WEEK 3

What I did this week to work on my goal:

WEEK 4

What I did this week to work on my goal:

I REACHED MY GOAL, SO I GET
_____

REACH THE GOAL!

My goal
_____

PROGRESS

WEEK 1
What I did this week to work on my goal:

WEEK 2
What I did this week to work on my goal:

WEEK 3
What I did this week to work on my goal:

WEEK 4
What I did this week to work on my goal:

I REACHED MY GOAL, SO I GET _____

REACH THE GOAL!

My goal _____

You made it!

What an awesome job you've done. I hope this journal has made you realise just how much you can achieve with the right mindset.

I would love to know which exercises you enjoyed most and any other feedback you have.

Please drop me a note at iona@30everafter.com. I'd love to hear from you.

Made in the USA
Coppell, TX
18 December 2019

13341608R00069